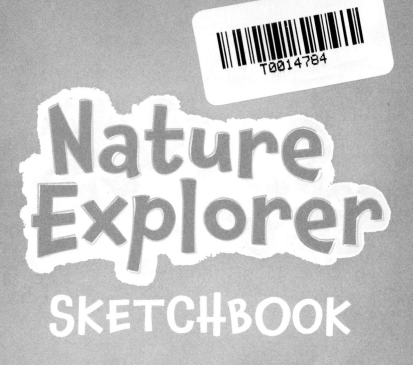

Nature Explorer
SKETCHBOOK

Jenny deFouw Geuder

PUBLICATIONS
Adventure
an imprint of AdventureKEEN

"All art starts small—whether it's a sketch of an eagle soaring or a painting of a wildflower. This sketchbook is yours for the art you want to make: whether you want to learn to draw birds, trace flowers, record your observations, or just doodle! Along the way, I'll provide occasional prompts and tips to guide you!"

Jenny deFouw Geuder

TIP

If something looks difficult to draw, try to simplify it to two or three basic shapes. The head might be a circle, the body an oval, and so on. Then look at the proportions of those shapes—how **BIG** is the body compared to the head?

Drawing is a lot like playing a sport: you have to teach your muscles how to work as a team with your eyes. The more you practice, the more you will get comfortable using your pencil, seeing an object proportionally, and recording it the way you want!

Try drawing many versions of the same thing: like lots of birds, different leaf shapes, different flowers, and so on.

Try using different materials than you usually do:
switch to a pen, or markers, or oil pastels.

Trying new things helps

you GROW as an artist.

TIP Try drawing something small really LARGE! Look for the little details.

TIP Try drawing just part of something, ZOOMED in.

Try drawing or painting the same spot,
but at different times of the day or year.

Don't be afraid of mistakes! Every "mistake" is a lesson—learn from it!

To get the best view of flowers or small features on dragonflies and the like, bring along a small magnifying glass. A digital camera can help too!

TIP One of the best ways to learn about plants is by making a leaf rubbing. Put a leaf under one of these pages, and gently use a charcoal pencil or a crayon to make a rubbing of the leaf.

Take your time

Find a spot with some flowers; sit for 5 minutes and pay attention. You might be surprised at the insects and animals you might have missed!

when you're observing.

Try different pencil techniques: hatching, crosshatching, stipple, scumble, and smooth shading.

hatching   crosshatching   stipple   scumble   smooth

Try holding your pencil in new ways to make different marks: hold it horizontally, under your hand, for shading. Hold it sideways and with your hand farther back for curved, sketch-like lines, and so on.

Look at the object you are drawing more than your drawing of it!

Try making a blind contour of a curved or crumpled leaf. To do so, sketch the shape (contour) of the leaf without looking at your paper. This takes practice, but it can be an effective way to draw.

Go to a zoo and sketch the animals you see: sketch quickly, no longer than 15 minutes, and label them. Try drawing them from different angles. Practice drawing animals that are close to you and mostly still. This will help you draw more quickly when you're out in the wild.

Record anything in nature that you find interesting: You see a cool leaf? Draw it. A beautiful feather? Draw it. Notice things!

Artists are

professional noticers.

TIP Try drawing one object, but from three different angles.

Squint your eyes a little when looking at your subject.
A good picture has a wide range of value (lights and darks),
and blurring your vision can help you see that.

Draw every day! Draw and draw and draw! As a beginner artist, try to use a reference (a photo of your subject or the real thing!) whenever possible. Draw from life.

TIP Perspective tips: things get smaller as they go away from you. If you want something to look farther away, draw it smaller (and higher on the page). Overlapping objects also gives depth.

When you're drawing a face: keep in mind that the eyes are usually halfway down the face. Artists often draw a "+" over a face to help them see where the eyes, nose, and other features should go.

eyes

nose

mouth

Fill these pages

with faces!

TIP Try not to use your finger to smudge your pencil, as that gets you dirty and puts oil from your fingers on your artwork. Instead, put a tissue over your finger when blending, or you can use a special tool called a "blending stump."

Practice gradients (color or shading transitions).
Color from light to dark with your pencil,
and try to color without adding streaks.
This is a great way to work on your shading skills.

TIP Use your eraser as a drawing tool! As you draw and shade things, use your eraser to pull out the highlights (areas where the light hits). Look carefully!

TIP

Use the Rule of Thirds to arrange your page: that means, pretend your picture has imaginary lines splitting it into thirds both up and down—put your focal point (the thing you want people to look at) at one of the intersections of those imaginary lines. Your pictures will be more interesting!

Don't judge your art against other people's work. Just have fun.
Every new skill takes time to learn, so enjoy the process!

TIP Look at where the light is coming from and add shadows on the other side! It will help your art look 3D.

Learn to compare

and spot differences.

Learn from other artists! Look around (online or at a museum) and find an artist you like. It doesn't matter if it's their style, their use of colors, or their subject that appeals to you. Then try to copy their work. Make sure you don't claim their work as yours, and write down their name to give them credit. Like this: Inspired by Vincent Van Gogh's *Starry Night*. All artists learn from others!

TIP If something is difficult to draw, try turning the picture upside down! It's an old artist's trick to help your brain see shapes and shadows instead of getting overwhelmed!

When you look at something, ask yourself questions. See what you notice, what an object reminds you of, and what you wonder about it.

ABOUT THE AUTHOR

Jenny deFouw Geuder is an artist and teacher from Michigan. She received her bachelor's and master's degrees in art education (and minored in English). She has been a middle school teacher for 16 years, and she's never stopped making art. She usually paints with watercolors, but she enjoys working with other paints and materials too. She lives in the country with her husband, two small boys, a dog, five cats, a hedgehog, chickens, and occasionally two ponies.

Cover and book design by Jonathan Norberg

Edited by Brett Ortler

Proofread by Emily Beaumont

Cover images copyright by Jenny deFouw Geuder except **Janine C./Shutterstock:** leaf rubbing; **KatMoy/Shutterstock:** background; and **ami mataraj/Shutterstock:** yellow circle.

Photo Credits:
Interior images copyright by Jenny deFouw Geuder.

Images purchased or sourced from the following stock sources:
Rolau Elena/Shutterstock: 4, 9, 24, 27, 38, 46, 56, 66, 71, 75, 78, 87, 90, 95, 97, 103, 110, 121 (TIP rectangle); **KatMoy/Shutterstock:** 1 (background); and **ami mataraj/Shutterstock:** 4, 9, 24, 27, 38, 46, 56, 66, 71, 75, 78, 87, 90, 95, 97, 103, 110, 121 (TIP circle).

Reference images for the following drawing used under license from Dreamstime.com: **Randall Runtsch:** 9 (bird drawing)

Author photo © 2023 by Josh Knap/Peninsula Photography

10 9 8 7 6 5 4 3 2 1
Nature Explorer Sketchbook
Copyright © 2023 by Jenny deFouw Geuder
Published by Adventure Publications
An imprint of AdventureKEEN
310 Garfield Street South
Cambridge, Minnesota 55008
(800) 678-7006
www.adventurepublications.net
All rights reserved
Printed in United States of America
ISBN 978-1-64755-376-0 (pbk.)